C000008314

100
FACTS

Rangers

First published in Great Britain in 2016
by Wymer Publishing
www.wymerpublishing.co.uk
Wymer Publishing is a trading name of Wymer (UK) Ltd

First edition. Copyright © 2016 David Clayton / Wymer Publishing.

ISBN 978-1-908724-17-5

Edited by Jerry Bloom.

Typeset by Andy Francis.
Printed and bound by CMP, Poole, Dorset

A catalogue record for this book is available from the British Library.

Cover design by Wymer.
Sketches by Becky Welton. © 2014.

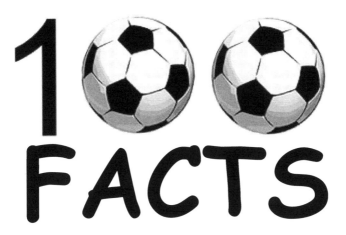

FACTS

Rangers

David Clayton

WYMER
PUBLISHING
Bedford, England

MOSES THE FIRST!

Moses McNeill was the first Rangers player to play international football and was also part of a group of friends who first discussed creating a football club in March 1872, though it was officially recognised as a club in 1873.

It was Moses who suggested the name 'Rangers' from an English rugby annual so his place in club folklore is assured!

McNeill would win just two caps in total and made his debut on 25th March 1876 as Scotland thrashed Wales 4-0 in the first match played between the two countries. It got better for McNeill, too as he rounded off a 100% record with his brother Henry playing alongside him in a 5-4 victory over England.

A powerful, stocky athlete, McNeill was involved in a number of firsts for Rangers – he played in the first ever Scottish Cup match during which he also scored in a 2-0 win over Oxford.

His last game was on 30th September 1882 when Rangers were beaten in a Scottish Cup replay away to Queen's Park, bringing to an end a 10-year playing career for the Club.

IN A LEAGUE OF THEIR OWN

Though the club had been active for several years, it wasn't until 1890 that the Gers played their first Scottish League match.

The Scottish Football League had been formed for the 1890/91 season and Rangers would play their games at Ibrox Stadium – not the one the club plays at today but an early version – and there were only 10 founding members who took part.

The historic first league match was played on 16th August 1890 and Rangers went on to beat Heart of Midlothian 5-2 – not a bad start!

It proved to be a decent season all round for Rangers who finished the campaign joint top with Dumbarton. Without goal difference or head-to-head stats to settle the argument, Rangers and Dumbarton took part in a play-off at Cathkin Park in Glasgow – a big park in the city – but the teams couldn't be separated and after a 2-2 draw, the title was shared for the only time in Scottish football history.

Presumably that meant the trophy being in one cabinet for six months and six months in another!

IBROX DISASTER (1902)

One of the saddest days in Glasgow Rangers Football Club's history occurred on 5th April, 1902 when 25 supporters were killed in what became known as 'The Ibrox Disaster'.

Rangers weren't actually playing that day – the ground was hosting a British Home Championship international match between Scotland and England at Ibrox Park.

The club has been proud of the construction of the new West Tribune Stand but the night before, torrential rain had fallen and weakened the structure. With the stand packed to watch the game, after 51 minutes of play the wooden stand collapsed under the weight of the people crammed into it. 25 people lost their lives and 517 people were injured, many of them badly hurt.

The investigation into the tragedy would result in the type of stand that had collapsed being banned from ever being built again.

From then on, stands either had to be built on a bank of earth to support the structure or be concrete based.

STANDING ROOM ONLY

Today's all-seater stadiums mean there is a controlled limit on how many people can attend matches and there are very good reasons why that is.

The safety of fans is the most important factor, but then you have policing, catering, parking and lots of other things to consider so things can be planned in advance and properly.

Ibrox Stadium's capacity today is 50,947 and no matter who Rangers play, the various departments know that's the maximum that can turn up – but it wasn't always that way!

Ibrox used to be a completely different design built for people to stand together on terraces. While this made for a great atmosphere, some stands were uncovered and can you imagine needing to go the toilet standing right in the middle of thousands of people?

So next time you're watching a match and nip to get a pie and a drink or bound up the gangway to the toilet, just imagine what it was like when a new British record was set at Ibrox as Rangers played Celtic.

A massive crowd of 118,567 fans crammed into the ground to create a League record that still stands today.

BEST OF ENEMIES

There are few derbies as fierce or passionate as the meeting of Glasgow giants Rangers and Celtic.

One of the most famous inter-city rivalries in world football, the fixture dates back to the first official meeting in 1888 and for many years the Glasgow derby has been known as 'The Old Firm' clash - though the exact reason it is called that is not known for sure.

People have made educated guesses and one theory is that commentators from the early Rangers v Celtic games may have referred to the rivals as being "like two old, firm friends".

The fact both clubs were among the original members of the Scottish Football League – the truth is, nobody can be certain!

One thing that is for sure is that Rangers and Celtic have always dominated Scottish football, sharing 101 top flight title triumphs between then along with 69 Scottish Cups and 42 Scottish League Cups - that means they've won more than 200 trophies in total!

The teams have also met more than 400 times in league and cups making it one of the most played fixtures anywhere in the world.

STAN THE MAN

It's a little-known fact that one of England greatest players, Sir Stanley Matthews, spent a brief time playing for Rangers.

Known as 'The Wizard of the Dribble', Matthews was best known for his time with Stoke City and Blackpool with whom he made combined appearances of nearly 800 games.

Matthews was considered as something of a genius and was a superstar of his day, representing England 54 times. So where do Rangers fit in to his glittering career?

Well, during World War II, football continued but it was very different from the League football that had taken place before the war.

Clubs played in regional leagues and played many friendlies and invited guests to represent them in certain games. Matthews, like other great players who weren't overseas fighting, accepted the offer to take part in one or two games and among them were Glasgow Rangers.

Matthews married the granddaughter of one the founding members of Rangers – Tom Vallance – so it was perhaps inevitable he would pull on a Gers shirt at some point.

Matthews played twice for Rangers, one of which was the Glasgow Charity Cup Final against Partick Thistle at Hampden Park.

PLAYER MANAGER

It's not easy to play and manage a football club which is why there have been so few who have made a great success of it.

It might also be why Rangers waited 113 years before employing their first player-manager! That man was Scottish international and former Liverpool legend Graeme Souness.

Souness arrived in 1986 after Rangers, who had sacked manager Jock Wallace, paid £300,000 for his services and at 33, he still had a season or two in him to contribute on the pitch.

Souness, a tough-tackling fiery character was regarded as one of the best midfielders of his generation and had won 54 caps for Scotland.

Though he would only play occasionally, he inspired Rangers to seven trophies in five years including 73 appearances and five goals.

Souness also stopped the drain of Scottish talent heading to England by bringing in several top English players which became big successes at Ibrox.

BAT AND BALL

Rangers have had two players who have represented the club and also been top cricketers.

Scot Symon was the first player to represent Scotland in football and cricket – he played against Hungary for Scotland in 1938 - his only cap - and was a top cricketer for Perthshire for several years.

Symon had played for Dundee and Portsmouth before joining his boyhood heroes Rangers in 1938. The war would sandwich his nine-year stay at Ibrox and the wing-half played just 37 times in total.

Symon played cricket for Scotland against Australia in 1938 taking five wickets for just 33 runs – quite an achievement – but he wasn't alone.

Rangers' goalkeeper Andy Goram played for the club from 1991 to 1998, representing his country on 43 occasions.

In 1989, he also played cricket for Scotland, with the right-arm medium paced bowler and batsman playing against Ireland and Australia and he also played two Nat West Trophy games for Scotland, too.

He remains the only person to have represented his country in a first class cricket match and a full football international.

GOALS GALORE!

The 1983 European Cup Winners' Cup saw Rangers go goal crazy.

The first round had paired the Gers with Maltese side Valetta and manager John Grieg knew his side had been given a relatively easy tie.

Valetta were one of the competition's weakest sides and teams from Malta traditionally lost heavily in European competition – and that pattern would continue.

The first leg in Malta attracted a crowd of 18,213 but Rangers' performance meant the majority of those fans went home disappointed after seeing Valetta thrashed 8-0 courtesy of goals from McPherson (4), Prytz (2), Paterson and MacDonald.

The second leg was a mere formality and that was reflected in the unusually low crowd of 11,500. Those who did attend saw Rangers in ruthless mood with the Maltese side again at the wrong end of another heavy defeat.

This time Rangers hit double figures, winning 10-0 to complete a record 18-0 aggregate victory. MacDonald helped himself to a hat-trick while Mitchell and Redford score twice each and there were also goals for Dawson, MacKay and Davies.

Despite the winning margin, the pressure on boss Grieg failed to ease and he resigned a month later.

FACT 10

One of Rangers' older nicknames may confuse some modern day fans.

Known in the early days as the 'Light Blues' the name is at odds with the team of today's royal blue jerseys.

The reason is pretty simple – Rangers' first kit consisted of a light blue shirt, white shorts and dark blue socks – hence the nickname!

In fact, the kit was not dissimilar to the colours of Manchester City and was worn – with some minor changes of sock colours – from 1893 until 1930.

After 1930, the Gers adopted the new royal blue shirt that has been the club's colours for the past 87 years (up to the 2016/17 campaign) and shows no sign of changing anytime soon.

If the home kit has been fairly consistent, the away kit has gone through a number of different versions ranging from all white, blue hoops, red shirts and white shorts plus blue and white stripes and even red and black striped shirts.

We won't even mention the orange third kit of 2002/03...

TWICE IN A DAY!

In the modern game managers often complain of playing too many games, particularly if there are two inside a week – so imagine what the reaction would have been to two games in one day?

Believe it or not, it actually happened in 1917 with the First World War meaning midweek games were banned leading to a major fixture congestion.

The only solution was to play twice in a day – something clubs agreed to so the 1916/17 season could end on schedule.

Rangers took on Hamilton Academicals in the first game, played at 3.30 on 21st April 1917 and lost 3-1.

Then it was a quick rush back to Ibrox to face Queen of the South who had also played just an hour or so earlier.

This time Rangers triumphed 1-0 in front of a crowd of approximately 7,000 to complete a busy afternoon! Rangers finished third that season behind Morton and champions Celtic.

Seven Rangers players played in both matches.

YOUNGEST PLAYER

Derek Ferguson is the youngest player to ever play for Rangers.

The Glasgow-born midfielder had barely turned 16 when he made his first-team debut against Queen of the South on 23rd August 1983.

Aged 16 years and 24 days old, Ferguson wrote his name into the history books with a record that will be hard to beat.

He went on to play 111 times for the club between 1983 and 1990, scoring seven goals in the process. But leaving Ibrox wasn't the end of his career – far from it!

Ferguson went on to play for another 13 clubs over the next 16 years – most notably at Hearts and Sunderland- and ended with career statistics of 475 games played but just 16 goals scored – an average of one goal every 29 games!

He won his only two Scotland caps in 1988 while with Rangers and the fact he hung his boots up in 2006 is testament to his longevity in football with a career spanning an amazing 23 years.

OLDEST PLAYER

The difference between Rangers' youngest player Derek Ferguson and the oldest, David Weir, is 25 years and 55 days.

Weir played for Rangers against Malmo on 26th July 2011 aged 41 years old and 77 days, but the majority of his career had been spent elsewhere.

Weir started out with hometown club Falkirk where the promising centre-back came to the attention of a number of other Scottish clubs and in 1996 he moved to Hearts for whom he would make 116 appearances for during a three-year period.

From 1998 to 2006 Weir played for Everton, playing more than 250 times for the Toffees before moving back to Scotland with Rangers.

He signed initially on a six-month deal with his age of 36 taken into consideration, but any doubt about his ability were soon dismissed and Weir rarely missed a game for the next five years before calling it a day after the Malmo game.

With 69 Scotland caps and 750 career appearances, Weir is deservedly regarded as a great of Scottish football and returned in 2015 to become Rangers' assistant manager.

ONE CLUB JOHN

When it comes to Rangers legends, there are few who can hold a candle to the great John Grieg who played his entire career at the club.

In 1999, he was voted 'The Greatest Ever Ranger' by supporters and few would disagree with that verdict.

Grieg was being courted by Hearts as a teenager but after watching them lose 6-1 to Edinburgh rivals Hibernian, he opted to take up Rangers' offer instead – a move he wouldn't regret.

Between 1961 and 1977, Grieg would make an incredible 755 appearances for Rangers scoring 120 goals.

He was a determined character and a great leader so it was inevitable he would skipper the team and during his 16 years as a player, Rangers won no less than 17 trophies.

He also captained Scotland on 15 occasions, winning 44 caps in total for his country.

Grieg returned to manage Rangers from 1978 to 1983, winning four cups but never managing to win the Scottish Premier League.

He has been in or around the club for most of his life and was awarded the MBE in 1977. Today, he is the Honorary Life President of Glasgow Rangers.

PENALTY KING

When it comes to masters of the spot-kick, nobody can beat Rangers' greatest ever penalty king Jimmy Hubbard.

Hubbard was born in South Africa and joined Rangers in 1949, remaining with the club for a decade.

A left-winger by trade, Hubbard could have joined Clyde instead, but despite being offered more money, he chose Rangers instead – a decision he wouldn't regret.

Hubbard was a popular figure among the fans and when he opted to start taking penalties, his popularity soared (even more so when he scored a hat-trick against Celtic!)

Hubbard would take 68 penalty kicks for the Gers and his conversion rate was hugely impressive scoring 65 of them.

Though he missed three, at one stage he banged in 22 in succession – an astonishing record and during the 1954/55 campaign, he ended top scorer with 27 goals – not bad for a left winger!

Hubbard left for Bury in 1959 having made 172 appearances and scored 77 goals – nobody has taken penalties quite as successfully at the club since.

Rangers became the first British club to compete in a European club final when the Gers went all the way in the 1960/61 inaugural European Cup Winners' Cup final.

The competition included just 10 teams, all champions in a domestic competition in their own country so by winning through just three rounds meant a place in the final.

The Light Blues first had to negate a preliminary round and so were paired with Hungarian side Ferencvaros, winning the first leg at Ibrox 4-2 and losing 2-1 in the return – though the hosts had led 2-0 at one point which would have taken them through on away goals.

That meant a ticket to the quarter-finals where the Gers were drawn against German side Borussia Monchengladbach but it proved to be much easier than anticipated with Rangers winning 3-0 in the away leg and 8-0 at Ibrox.

Next up was the battle of Britain as Rangers played English side Wolverhampton Wanderers, winning the home leg 2-0 and drawing 1-1 in the return.

Italian side Fiorentina were all that stood in the way of Rangers winning the competition, but this time things didn't go the way of the Gers.

Fiorentina weren't intimidated by the 80,000 Ibrox crowd and won 2-0, completing the job with a 2-1 win in Florence – it was the only time the final was contested over two legs.

FACT 17

So you've heard of a penalty shoot-out to settle a match? Or maybe extra time to find a winner? You may have heard of the Golden Goal rule (first to score in extra time) or even tossing a coin (yes, this actually happened a number of times!)

There have been numerous ways to find a winning team but in the 1942/43 Southern League season, the Light Blues were both the beneficiaries and victims of a unique way of deciding a tied game.

Having drawn a Scottish League Cup tie with Falkirk 1-1 at Hampden Park, some bright spark had agreed that, in the event of a draw, corners would be counted to decide the outcome.

It was a bizarre decision, but as Rangers had 11 to Falkirk's 3, nobody from Glasgow was complaining.

However, the method would come back to haunt the Gers in the final, when, after drawing 0-0 with Hibernian, the corner count came into play and this time it was the Edinburgh side that had the last laugh after winning 6-5 to win the cup – harsh!

GOLDEN ALLY

No Rangers striker has scored more goals than Ally McCoist who banged in an incredible 355 during his time at Ibrox.

There seemed little of the goal-machine that was to come in McCoist's early days. As a teenager, his first two seasons with St Johnstone saw him fail to find the net even once, though his first full campaign saw him score 23 goals in 43 games.

That convinced Sunderland to pay a club record £400,000 for the promising striker and a few games into the 1981/82 he moved to Roker Park.

The move, however, never really sparked the best in McCoist who struggled with the expectation that such a large fee brought with it and with just nine goals from 65 appearances, Rangers paid £185,000 to take him back to Scotland.

McCoist never looked back and for the next 15 years, he was an Ibrox idol, breaking numerous club records in the process.

He hit double figures in each of his seasons with Rangers apart from one injury hit campaign and his best return was 49 goals from 52 appearances in 1992/93.

All told, he finished with 355 from 581 appearances – phenomenal!

A hat-trick is a fantastic achievement for any player - Ally McCoist has scored the most trebles for Rangers, taking the match ball home on no less than 28 occasions!

But some achievements eclipse even banging in three, and one player in particular managed this very special feat not once, but twice within the space of 12 months.

That man is Jimmy Smith and though McCoist is the Light Blues' official top scorer, Smith played throughout the war years - which the record books don't count - and scored 382 goals in 411 starts! Smith's unique record was scoring six goals, twice in a match inside 361 days between 1933 and 1934.

The first double hat-trick was in a 9-1 win over Ayr United in August 1933 and almost exactly a year later he scored six goals in a 7-1 win over Dunfermline Athletic.

Smith's career spanned 18 years at Ibrox and he won 24 winners' medals during that time - no wonder he is remembered as a club legend and there will be probably never be a Rangers striker as prolific as Smith again.

Some strikers go a few games without scoring or have a season when they don't score that many goals at all.

In fact, it's not common for a striker to just about reach double figures – so how about if you scored almost a season's worth of goals in one game? That's what happened in 1934 when Jimmy Fleming scored three hat-tricks in one game!

Fleming's famous feat came during a Scottish Cup victory over tiny amateur club Blairgowrie when Rangers secured a club record 14-2 victory.

It's the most goals scored by Rangers in a match and Fleming broke a host of club and national records when he scored his nine goals.

Fleming had signed from St Johnstone and he ended his time with the club having scored 44 Scottish Cup goals.

For the record, Fleming scored his first goal in the first minute and his ninth in the 89th minute and ended the season with 26 goals from 19 starts. His overall record for Rangers was 231 goals in 278 matches.

There are several notable records for Rangers players connected with the World Cup.

The first player to ever appear in the competition was Eric Cadlow when played against Yugoslavia in the 1958 World Cup.

At the same tournament, Sammy Baird scored the first goal by a Rangers player at the World Cup when he found the net against France a week later.

With Scotland's appearances at the World Cup few and far between, it's no surprise that the most appearances for a Rangers player is relatively low – Sandy Jardine played four times – more than any other player from the club.

Only two Rangers players have ever managed to score in the World Cup – as earlier mentioned, Baird is one of them with Mo Johnstone the other.

Plenty of scope for those records to be broken in years to come!

While we're on international duty, Rangers most capped player while with the club is Ally McCoist with 60 appearances and he is also the top scorer for the club, managing 19 goals for his country while at Ibrox.

INTO THE WOODS

Goalkeeper Chris Woods arrived at Ibrox in 1986 and would have a first season to remember as he set not only a new record for Rangers, but a British record during a remarkable run.

Between November 1986 and January 1987 Woods didn't concede a single goal for 1196 minutes – the equivalent of 13.2 consecutive matches.

The former Nottingham Forest and England keeper was finally beaten by Adrian's Sprott's goal for Hamilton Academicals who beat Rangers 1-0 at Ibrox in a Scottish Cup match.

Woods enjoyed a fine career, starting off at Nottingham Forest where he had Peter Shilton ahead of him and then moving on to QPR.

In 1981 he moved to Norwich City and spent five years at Carrow Road before Rangers paid £600,000 for his services.

He stayed in Scotland for five years before he was replaced by Andy Goram and the 43-times capped custodian was sold to Sheffield Wednesday for £1.2 million.

CHAMPIONS!

No club, not even fierce rivals Celtic can match Rangers for silverware.

The Gers have won the Scottish top tier title – today called the Scottish Premier League - more times than anyone else and have been runners-up on 30 occasions and third more than any other team in Scotland too!

Going into the 2016/17 season, Rangers had won the title 54 times – that's seven times more than closest rivals Celtic who have 47 championships under their belt.

The longest sequence of title successes was between 1988 and 1997 when the Light Blues won nine SPL crowns on the bounce – quite an achievement.
It matched the same feat Celtic had managed between 1965 and 1974.

Glasgow has dominated football in Scotland, with the title coming back to the city 101 times from a possible 120 compared with Edinburgh whose two teams have won the championship on just eight occasions (Hearts x4 and Hibernian x4). Aberdeen have also been champions four times.

It's now 31 years since a team outside of Glasgow won the SPL with Aberdeen triumphing back in 1985. That's some record...

Rangers have only won one major European trophy to date.

In 1972, the club lifted the European Cup Winners' Cup but it was far from an easy journey. The adventure began in the first round against French side Rennes, and after securing a 1-1 draw in France before edging a narrow 1-0 win at Ibrox.

The second round matches against Sporting Lisbon were packed with thrills and drama as the tie

swung one way, then the other though it looked as though it would be plain sailing for the Gers after opened up a 3-0 after just 30 minutes of the first leg.

However, two second half goals by the Portuguese side completely changed the complexion of the tie and Rangers had to fight tooth and nail in the return, losing 4-3 in extra time to progress on away goals.

A hard-fought 2-1 aggregate win over Torino in the quarter-finals set up a semi against the mighty Bayern Munich.

Rangers battled hard for a 1-1 draw in Germany before 80,000 Ibrox fans saw goals from Sandy Jardine and Derek Parlane secure a 2-0 win.

The final against Dynamo Moscow at the Nou Camp in Barcelona saw Rangers race into a 3-0 lead with 49 minutes gone and though the Russians pulled two goals back, the Gers held out for a famous victory.

Nine players wrote their names into Rangers history and probably didn't know that much about it at the time.

With the Light Blues scoring more than 9,000 goals in competitive games since the start of the club's history, nine notable milestones have been reached.

Alex Smith scored the 1,000th league goal against Clyde in 1906 and 13 years later, Jimmy Gordon scored the 2,000th against Kilmarnock in 1919.

It was an 11-year wait until the 3,000th goal went in when Bob McGowan scored against Cowdenbeath during a 7-0 win in 1930.

The war meant it was another 17 years until the 4,000th goal was scored when Jimmy Duncanson scored in a 3-1 win over Dundee.

Fourteen years passed until goal number 5,000 was scored – Alex Scott's effort in a 7-3 win over Ayr United, but it took only 13 more years to reach the 6,000 mark as Derek Parlane scored in a 4-2 victory over Hearts.

Ally McCoist grabbed goal number 7,000 as he bagged one against Motherwell 15 years after Parlane in 1989 and Shota Arveladze scored the 8,000th in 2002.

The last time a player reached a millennium was in October 2014 when Lee McCulloch scored goal 9,000 in a 6-1 in over Raith.

Based on the average of around 13 years the 10,000 landmark should be reached in around 2027.

BAD DAYS AT THE OFFICE

Every club has a skeleton in their closet - a fact they'd rather not remember – but, as in this case, every team has suffered heavy defeats and Rangers are no different.

The worst pasting the Gers have suffered came in a friendly when Airdrie won 10-2 in 1886, but as it was an unofficial match, it isn't the official heaviest defeat.

A 6-0 thrashing by Dumbarton in 1892 is etched into history and the worst loss in European competition came when Real Madrid scored six without reply in October 1963.

Sadly, the worst official defeat was against Celtic. Worse still, it came at Hampden Park in the 1957 Scottish League Cup final played in front of 82,293 fans.

It was a day every Rangers fan would like erased from history but it was just a match when everything went wrong for the Light Blues and everything went right for the Hoops.

With 44 minutes gone, it was only 1-0 to Celtic, but once the second went in before the break, Rangers were up against it and even though Billy Simpson reduced the deficit to 3-1 but four goals in the last 23 minutes completed the rout.

Ouch!

TRANSFER RECORDS
IN AND OUT

The most money Rangers have received for a player was when Tottenham Hotspur paid £9million for Alan Hutton in 2008.

That broke an eight-year record held by Giovanni van Bronckhorst who left Ibrox for Arsenal for £8.5 million.

Other notable fees received include the £8m fee paid by Newcastle United in January 2005 and more recently, the £7.8m Aston Villa invested in Carlos Cuellar in 2008.

Barry Ferguson joined Blackburn Rovers for £7.5m in 2003 and a year before Tore Andre Flo left Ibrox for Sunderland.

As for transfer fees paid by Rangers, the £12m record paid to Chelsea for Tore Andre Flo in 2000 has held for 16 years.

That fee is almost double the next highest of £6.5m paid to Everton for full-back Michael Ball while the biggest amount of money paid for a Scottish player was the £4.5m Rangers spent on bringing Barry Ferguson back to the club after just two years in England.

No doubt in years to come both the record transfer fee paid and the record transfer fee received will be broken – watch this space!

MERCHANTS OF GLASGOW

Between 1877 and 1966, Rangers took part in the Glasgow Merchants Cup – a charity knockout tournament initially open to teams in and around Glasgow.

As time went on the Glasgow Charity Cup Committee would invite clubs to take part – but whoever took part knew they would have to, at some stage, get past Rangers or Celtic and so the two city rivals dominated proceedings winning the cup 59 times between them.

Of that figure, Rangers have won the most though towards the end of its life, it became a one-off contest between a Glasgow Select side and a team invited from England.

It was Queen's Park who dominated the Merchants Cup in the early years winning ten of the first 13 cups – in fact, Rangers won it just once out of the first 20 attempts, though made up for it thereafter.

By the time Rangers won the competition for the final time in 1960, the Light Blues had registered 31 triumphs and been runners-up on 20 occasions while Celtic had managed 28 wins.

Rangers contested the very first European Super Cup in 1972 – or did they?

The idea was that the winners of the European Cup would play the winners of the European Cup Winners' Cup in a battle to be named top dogs in Europe, but though those teams were Ajax and Rangers, UEFA rejected the plan as fans of the Light Blues were serving a one-year ban for alleged misbehaviour.

However, you can't keep a good idea down so the contest was played over two legs anyway, but under the guise of Rangers' centenary celebrations!

The first match went ahead on 16th January 1973 at Ibrox and attracted a crowd of 58,000, but the Dutch side, packed with quality, skill and guile – not to mention the late, great Johan Cruyff, won the first leg 3-1.

The second encounter in Amsterdam's Olympic Stadium eight days later was an entertaining affair that, for a time, looked like Rangers might go on and win.

Leading 2-1 with 35 minutes played, Ajax pulled the match around, winning 3-2 on the night and 6-3 overall to the delight of 43,000 Ajax supporters.

So while UEFA didn't recognise the matches, it is widely regarded as the very first European Super Cup final.

RANGERS AND THE FA CUP

Rangers in the English FA Cup? Surely not!

Yes, in 1886/87 the Light Blues entered the FA Cup along with a host of other Scottish Cup and were drawn at home to Everton in the First Round.

The tie, however never went ahead through no fault of Rangers and as a result, Gers were handed a walkover which meant they progressed to the second round.

Drawn at home to interestingly named 'Church', Rangers turned in a heavenly display (of sorts) to win 2-1 and make the third round.

Rangers were again drawn at home and this time faced fellow Scots Cowlairs, winning 3-2. Whatever the fourth round was meant to be, it involved no games and Rangers received a bye to round 5 – the last 16.

Yet to leave Scotland, Rangers drew Lincoln City at home and beat the English side 3-0 to progress to the quarter-finals where – again at home (!) – Rangers beat Old Westminsters 5-1 to set up a semi-final with Aston Villa.

This time, the Gers' luck finally ran out as they lost 3-1 to Villa who went on to win the final beating West Brom 2-0.

TICKETS PLEASE!

There are many reasons why people leave matches early.

Perhaps the most common is they aren't happy with what they are watching and if there team has little chance of coming back and getting a result, heading for the exits seems like a good idea.

Sometimes the thought of getting stuck in the traffic after the game is reason enough to get a head start – as mentioned, there are many reasons.

But what if the tables were turned and one of the teams decided to leave early?

Impossible? Well – as you may have guessed – it did happen to Rangers on one occasion. It happened during a Glasgow Merchants Charity Cup tie at Second Hampden in April 1888.

The Light Blues were taking on Vale of Leven and leading 5-3 in front of a crowd just shy of 4,000 people when the team were summoned off with ten minutes still remaining.

The mystified supporters wondered what was happening but the reason was Vale of Leven needed to catch the Alexandria train so they packed up and headed for the station!

The result stood and Rangers won the match and safe to say an incident like this has never been recorded since.

Nothing like forward planning, eh?

FAMOUS FANS

Rangers have their fair share of celebrity supporters with a good mix of actors, sportsmen and celebrities.

Perhaps the most famous of all is 007 himself, James Bond star Sean Connery who actually started out as a Celtic fan! Golfing legend Arnold Palmer, winner of countless top tournaments (14 majors) is another fan of the Light Blues as is another top golfer, South African Gary Player. Colin Montgomerie makes for an impressive trio of golfing superstars.

Actor Robert Carlyle is a huge fan of the Gers as is former Ultravox singer Midge Ure who helped organise Band Aid and Live Aid.

TV super chef Gordon Ramsey is a passionate Rangers fans and in 1984, had a trial with the club, though the closest he got to the first team was a testimonial game against East Kilbride – an injury in training meant his chance ended soon after.

There are many more – too numerous to mention them all – but football fans will recognise the name of Jim White – Sky Sports News' legendary transfer deadline day anchor-man is another famous face sometimes spotted at Ibrox.

GREEK TRAGEDY?

Probably the day all proud Scottish Rangers fans dreaded became a reality in 2003 when the Light Blues took on Panathinaikos in a Champions League tie in Athens.

For the first time in the club's history, Rangers fielded a starting XI that didn't include one Scotsman!

The founding fathers would surely be turning in their grave...

Rangers came away with a creditable 1-1 draw for this historic fixture and, for the record, the starting eleven and their nationalities were as follows:

Stefan Klos (Germany)
Zurab Khizanishvili (Georgia)
Craig Moore (Australia)
Henning Berg (Norway)
Michael Ball (England)
Nuno Capucho (Portugal)
Mikel Arteta (Spain)
Emerson (Brazil)
Peter Lovenkrands (Denmark)
Michael Mols (Netherlands)
Shota Avreladze (Georgia)
Subs:
Paolo Vanoli (Italy)
Christian Nerlinger (German)

In 2012, the unthinkable happened as Rangers were kicked out of the Scottish Premier League and demoted to the Scottish League Two – the third tier of Scottish football.

With millions owed in taxes, a European ban and players not being paid, the club were in meltdown with many leaving at the end of the season and the club – who were bought out by a new consortium – were liquidated meaning their membership to the SPL and SFA lapsed.

The takeover had come too late with other clubs angered that Rangers may be allowed to continue unpunished and amid severe pressure from other clubs and their supporters, Rangers were demoted to the bottom league as punishment.

As expected, Rangers, who couldn't buy any new players in their first season, were promoted at the first attempt and made it back-to-back promotions the following season to move within one promotion of a return to the top flight.

However the club's problems were still causing issues behind the scenes and Rangers hopes of making it back in the quickest possible time and were defeated by Motherwell in the Championship play-off.

A year later, however, Rangers secured the second tier title to return to their rightful place in the top division.

CHAMPIONS OF CHAMPIONS

No club in world football has won as many trophies as Rangers, officially the most honoured club in world football.

With 117 trophies to date, Rangers are a class apart when it comes to silverware and have one of the most packed trophy rooms of any club you care to name.

With 54 top-flight titles, 33 Scottish Cup triumphs and 27 Scottish League Cup victories, domestically, it's rare a season passes without Rangers winning something.

The club became the first in world football to reach the 50 trophies milestone and they were first again to post the 100 titles won record.

If you add the European Cup Winners' Cup triumph, it's not a bad record though any Rangers fan would admit they would have preferred to have been a bigger power in European football.

To the above add 48 Glasgow Cup successes, 32 Glasgow Merchants Charity Cup wins, four Southern League Cup triumphs and a 2016 Challenge Cup win and you are looking at 200-plus in terms of silverware won – an amazing record and a source of great pride to all fans of the Light Blues.

GLASGOW CUP

Like the Glasgow Merchants Charity Cup, the Glasgow Cup was a trophy created for the teams of Glasgow to compete in which meant Rangers, Celtic, Clyde, Partick Thistle and Queen's Park. Third Lanark, who no longer exist, also competed during the Glasgow Cup's halcyon days.

The knockout competition ran from 1887 until 1989, with interest gradually fizzling out over the years.

It will come as no surprise to learn that Rangers and Celtic have dominated the cup with the Light Blues registering 48 triumphs compared to Celtic's 34.

In fact, the competition became so irrelevant to clubs that it wasn't even completed on several occasions with clubs unable to squeeze the fixtures into their busy programme.

In its early days, the cup was a source of great city pride and regarded as highly as the other cup competitions of the day.

The last time it received real prominence was in 1986 when Rangers beat Celtic 3-2 courtesy of an Ally McCoist hat-trick in front of more than 40,000 fans – thereafter it became little more than a reserve team cup.

THE IBROX DISASTER (1971)

Ibrox suffered its second major disaster in 1971 and this one was even worse than the tragedy of 1902 that saw 26 people killed when a wooden stand collapsed.

On this occasion, the Light Blues were taking on Celtic in an Old Firm derby. There had been warnings of danger in previous years with two people killed on Stairway 13 in 1961 during a crush on the stairwell.

Others were injured in later years and many believe it was a tragedy waiting to happen, but like all disasters, it was the chain of events that happened moments before that contributed to events,

With 80,000 packed inside, Celtic took a 90th minute lead and many fans decided to leave believing Rangers would lose the game. But when an injury time equaliser was scored, the problems really began.

Did fans who had left run back up Stairway 13, colliding with those exiting – the investigations suggested not as everyone had been facing the same way when they fell. Did one person's fall cause a domino effect that ended with hundreds of people falling on those further down the stairs?

Nobody is quite sure, but the end result was 66 people were killed in the crush and more than 200 injured – many of them children. It was a black day in the club's history and it took many years for fans and Rangers FC to come to terms with such a huge loss of life.

THE WAR YEARS

For six years, football stood still between 1940 and 1946 as Britain and her allies fought Germany in the second world conflict.

All Wartime matches were recorded, but did not count towards official statistics as the threat of attack meant the leagues and competitions were suspended, replaced by tournaments that existed only during that period.

Rangers had a team that continued playing, but it differed from the side that had played before the war and often included several 'guest' players.

Rangers continued to be successful, winning seven Southern League Championships, four Southern League Cups plus the Victory Cup, Emergency War Cup and the Summer Cup – in many ways, business as usual for the club! New Year's Day 1943 was also particularly pleasing as Rangers thrashed Celtic 8-1 and in November 1945, more than 95,000 saw Rangers draw 2-2 with Moscow Dynamo.

Several players were away fighting for their nation and Willie Thornton won a Military Medal for his bravery in Sicily.

Other Rangers players whose careers were put on hold to fight for their country were Davie Kinnear, Tom McKillop, James Galloway, Ian McPherson, Chis McNee, Eddie Rutherford, Billy Williamson, Alastair McKillop, David Marshall, Willie Paton and Jimmy Parlane.

FIRST WORLD WAR HEROES

Rangers lost five players during the World War One. The five heroes died in battle defending their country and are a source of great pride for the club and for Britain.

The first to fall was David Murray who was killed in action on October 6th 1915 and is buried at a Military Cemetery in France.

John Fleming was 26 when he was killed in March 1916 – he was brought home and is buried in Midlothian.

In August 1917 James Speirs lost his life during fighting in Belgium and he is buried close to where he fell in Zonnebecke.

Corporal Alex Barrie was killed in action in October 1918 and is buried in Northern France and Walter Tull died at the Second Battle of the Somme.

Several players were also wounded in action including Finlay Speedie, Tommy Muirhead, John Clarke, John Bovill, James Paterson, John McCulloch, James Galt and Willie Koivlichan – heroes every one of them.

From 17th August 1920 to April 26th 1954, Bill Struth was manager of Rangers. He was also the club's greatest and most successful boss during his 34 years in charge.

It was an incredible stint beginning with a 4-1 win over Airdrie and ending with a 2-2 draw with Hibs. Struth was a tough, uncompromising boss who had served as trainer under previous manager William Wilton for six years before taking the helm.

His time at Ibrox was incredibly successful and it was under Struth that Rangers became a football powerhouse as he guided the Light Blues to an incredible 25 top flight titles and his overall haul of trophies was in excess of 80 and included 10 Scottish Cups and two Scottish League Cups.

Struth's overall record was 1576 games as manager, 1089 of which were victories. There were also 288 draws and just 199 defeats during his mammoth career at Ibrox.

He retired as manager after the Hibs draw in 1954 aged 79 and became a club director for two years up until his death in 1956.

Rangers are unlikely to ever have a manager as successful as Bill Struth again.

ANNAN ATHLETIC

For many Rangers fans the lowest the club has ever sunk was during the 2012/13 Scottish Division Three campaign.

Having begun the long journey to try and regain the club's Scottish Premier League status, the Light Blues embarked on a league campaign against a host of teams they'd never played before – one of them, Annan Athletic, proved particularly troublesome.

The first meeting at Annan's Galabank stadium was an indication of what was to come as the hosts fought out a bruising 0-0 draw, much to the delight of the home supporters.

Normal service seemed to have resumed when the teams met again in mid-December with Rangers winning 3-0 at Ibrox and a fortnight later, the Gers started 2013 with a 3-1 win at Galabank.

Seven points out of a possible nine was a decent return for Ally McCoist's men, but the truth was Rangers were just about doing enough.

Then, in front of a large Ibrox crowd, Annan recoded the biggest win in their history with a 2-1 win at Ibrox

Rangers did win the title and Annan finish third bottom, but it was a painful reminder of how far and quickly the Glasgow giants had fallen.

Walter Tull never actually played competitive football for Rangers, but his place in the club's history is assured.

The son of a Barbadian carpenter played for Tottenham and Northampton Town and he was responsible for a number of firsts for many clubs and the British Army, for whom he would become the first black infantry officer.

In 1917, while he was training to be an officer in Scotland, his ability as a footballer came to the attention of Rangers and Tull signed to play for the club once the war had ended, technically becoming the Light Blues' first black player.

A remarkable young man who opened the door for so many others, Tull's parents both died when he was a young boy and he was sent to an orphanage where he was adopted by the Warnock family of Glasgow.

While playing for Spurs, he became the first mixed-heritage professional to play in South America and was also the first mixed race player to appear in the top division – one of numerous historic landmarks.

Sadly, Tull would never appear for Rangers as he died a hero during the German Spring Offensive in World War One – but his legacy lives on.

Rangers' first match was played on Glasgow Green 1872 and thereafter the fledgling club played football on public pitches across the city. The first regular venue was called Burnbank, and Rangers played there during 1875.

The first home ground of any real note was Kinning Park – Clydesdale cricket ground which, after improvements, housed 7,000 fans and the Light Blues stayed as tenants until 1887 when, after issues with the landlords, the club shared Third Lanark's Cathkin Park.

Rangers move to the area of Ibrox in 1887 and named their first purpose-built home Ibrox Park which had a 15,000 capacity and the club remained happy there, hosting three international fixtures as well as the 1890 Scottish Cup Final. But in December 1899 –with Celtic Park a bigger and more advanced ground, pressure was on the Gers to play catch-up.

By becoming a limited company, the club raised funds that enabled the new Ibrox Park to open on 30th December 1899 and by 1902 had a capacity of 75,000.

The ground remained as Ibrox Park until 1997 when it simply became Ibrox and over a number of years, the ground became an all-seater stadium and today has a capacity of 50,947.

CONN MAN

Alfie Conn became the first post-war player to play for both Rangers and Celtic – a hugely controversial move at the time and to some extent, the same applies for any player who dares to switch sides in Glasgow.

A flamboyant, cultured midfielder, Conn started out at Ibrox, making his debut in the predecessor for the UEFA Cup tie in November 1968 and became an integral member of the team over the next few years, playing in the 1972 European Cup Winners' Cup triumph of 1972.

He also scored in a 3-2 Scottish Cup final win over Celtic in 1973 before moving to Tottenham Hotspur where he would stay from 1974 to 1977, becoming a firm favourite with the fans during his time in North London.

In 1977 he joined Celtic and was part of the side that beat Rangers 1-0 in the Scottish Cup final, but he only remained at Parkhead for two years. The move didn't go down well with Rangers fans who had trouble understanding his defection to 'the other side'.

That said, he was later inducted into the Rangers Hall of Fame, so the damage wasn't quite irreparable!

Former Manchester United manager Alex Ferguson stopped by at Ibrox during his playing career.

He spent the first 10 years of his career with Queen's Park, Dunfermline and St Johnstone and was a prolific striker for each side he played for.

At the age of 26 Rangers paid a record £65,000 to bring Ferguson to the club where he would stay between 1967 and 1969.

It was the largest transfer fee paid between two Scottish clubs at the time and Ferguson wouldn't disappoint with a goal return of 44 goals in 57 appearances.

Ferguson used to collect the teenage Kenny Dalglish – future Liverpool legend and manager - and take him into town when the young forward was looking for a club – he would later join Celtic and end up marking Ferguson in the role of centre-back during a reserve game!

Things went sour for Ferguson when he was blamed for losing Celtic skipper Billy McNeill when he was supposed to be marking him with Celtic going on to win the game.

Forced to train with the youngsters as punishment and upset at his treatment, Ferguson reportedly threw away his losers' medal.

As a result of the fall out, Ferguson joined Falkirk and later Ayr United before moving on to an incredibly successful management career with Aberdeen and then Manchester United.

TITLE DECIDER

The 1904/05 Scottish Division One campaign couldn't have been closer with Celtic and Rangers finishing level at the top on 41 points,

Under today's rules, the fact that Rangers had a better goal difference and had won 19 games to Celtic's 18 would mean the Light Blues would be crowned champions, but back then, there was no way of separating the teams and the only option was to have a play-off.

Hampden Park was the venue for the most important Old Firm clash yet but things went Celtic's way in front of 30,000 fans, with goals from McMenemy and Hamilton with Robertson scoring Rangers' only goal.

The victory saw Celtic crowned champions – their first title in seven years.

The details from this historic match are:

CELTIC 2- 1 RANGERS
6th May 1905, Hampden Park

CELTIC: Adams - McLeod, Orr - McNair, Loney, Hay - Bennett, McMenemy, Quinn, Somers, Hamilton.

RANGERS: Sinclair - Fraser, Craig - Gourlay, Stark, May - Robertson, Speedie, McColl, Donaghy, Smith.

THE PERFECT SEASON

The 1898/99 season was a perfect campaign by the Light Blues who won every league game.

Secretary William Wilton oversaw the season during which Rangers won all 18 matches to win the league in a canter.

With 79 goals scored and just 18 conceded, the Gers averaged a score (more or less) of 4-1 in every game they played.

It was a time when a win meant just two points, not three and saw Rangers finish 10 points clear of second placed Hearts.

Wilton's side began as it meant to go on, beating Partick Thistle 6-2 with Robert Hamilton, who would go on to score 21 goals, bagging a hat-trick.

The 100% record seemed to be coming to an end in game 11 when Hibs went into a 2-0 lead – Rangers pulled it back to 2-2 before falling behind again. Back came the Gers again to make it 3-3 and then, with the final act of the game, Neil struck home a last-gasp penalty to win the game 4-3.

In the return game, Rangers thrashed Hibs 10-0 – perhaps for almost ruining their record earlier in the season!

Celtic were beaten 4-0 and 4-1, and the final game against Clyde was a nervy affair for the players and supporters but Clyde were eventually overcome on an icy January afternoon with Rangers winning 3-0.

Nobody scored more goals against Celtic than Rangers striker Robert Hamilton – also known as R.C Hamilton.

Rangers captain Hamilton scored 31 goals against the Hoops during his nine-year stay with the club and his overall record of 154 goals in 164 games is nothing short of sensational.

Hamilton began life with his local team Elgin City in the Highland League before joining Queen of the South in 1896.

A move to Glasgow to attend university saw Hamilton sign for Rangers a year later where his career really took off.

A prolific striker with a fierce long range shot, he would finish top scorer in each of his nine seasons for the Light Blues and he won four titles and two Scottish Cup triumphs as well.

Hamilton would win 11 Scotland caps in total, scoring 15 goals and in 1906 he moved south to join Fulham.

He remained in West London for one season before returning for one more year at Rangers, but then moved on to Morton, Hearts, Dundee and finally Elgin City before hanging his boots up for good.

His Old Firm record has stood for more than 100 years.

WILLIAM THE GREAT

William Wilton was Rangers' first manager and one of the most successful too.

But for a tragic accident he may have gone on to win many more titles.

Wilton arrived at the club as a player in September 1883 but never made it past the Second XI. A popular and intelligent man, he was given the role of secretary – an early version of the manager for the youth and reserve side and was part of the management team that helped the club find its first home at Ibrox.

Wilton was promoted to match secretary for the first team in 1889 and Rangers shared the first league title in the inaugural season for Scottish football. He also became league treasurer in 1891.

After a decade with the club Wilton proudly accepted the role of becoming Rangers' first manager and under his reign, the Light Blues won eight league titles, the Scottish Cup plus 16 other trophies.

Sadly, Wilton was killed in a boating accident the day after his team lifted a tenth title in just 11 years – an incredible record.

His death paved the way for his trainer Bill Struth to take over and went on to even greater success in a period of sustained success for Rangers – although Wilton's loss was a huge blow to the club.

HOME FROM HOME

Between 1909 and 2014 Scotland have played 22 international matches at Ibrox.

Between 1889 and 1897 the national team also played three games at Ibrox Park, the Light Blues' first proper home ground.

Celtic Park has held 25 internationals and next behind Rangers is Aberdeen's Pittodrie Stadium.

The last time Scotland played at Ibrox was October 2014 when 34,719 fans saw a 1-0 win over Georgia.

Prior to that, Scotland beat Bosnia 1-0 in 1999 thanks to a John Collins penalty in front of just over 30,000 fans.

Scotland's overall record at Ibrox is quite impressive with 15 wins, three draws and just four losses to date, scoring 50 goals and conceding just 13.

Rangers have won the Scottish Cup on 33 occasions, starting with a first success in 1893/94 when Celtic were beaten 3-1.

From 1934 to 1936 Rangers won the cup three times in a row and repeated the feat straight after the war, from 1948 to 1950.

It was three in a row again between 1962 and 1964.

As for successful decades, the 1930s, 1960s and 2000s all resulted with five Scottish Cup wins and since the cup began, only the 1910s saw Rangers fail to win the cup and the 1980s saw just one success.

Rangers' last success was in 2009 with a 1-0 win over Falkirk.

The Light Blues have also been runners-up on 17 occasions including four in the 1980s – a grand total of 50 finals in total up to the end of the 2015/16 campaign.

ON YER BIKE!

One of Rangers' fans' favourite trophy room items is the bike that is randomly parked under a painting of William Struth.

It's one of the first questions people ask when they see it, seemingly out of place and perhaps left by a member of staff!

The bike is a treasured gift from French club St Etienne, who played Rangers in a 1957 European Cup tie.

Before the match St Etienne presented the bike to the club. It was a replica of a Tour de France winner's cycle who had connections with the French city.

Rangers won the home tie 3-1 and lost 2-1 in the return to progress to the next round.

The teams would meet again in 1975 with St Etienne avenging the loss 18 years earlier but the French side again presented a unique gift – a French miner's lamp – which also still resides in the trophy room.

So if you ever visit Ibrox and pop into the trophy room and hear someone say, 'Why's there a bike in here?', you can explain why it's there and where it came from.

Now the clock Ajax presented is a totally different story...

FLYING START

A fledgling Rangers had just four years to wait until their first major cup final.

The Light Blues were a young and vibrant side just making their way in the game but in 1877 Rangers went all the way to the final where they would face the more experienced and physically stronger Vale of Leven, also playing in their first final.

The first attempt at settling the final saw Rangers hold Vale of Leven to a 1-1 draw at Hampden Crescent watched by 8,000 fans.

The plucky Gers then held Leven again in the replayed final, again at Hampden Crescent with the score the same as the first game. More than 15,000 turned up for this game, suggesting Rangers were stating the get a decent following in Glasgow.

The third game saw Rangers again battle hard, but this time Vale of Leven edged the game by 3-2 in a match played at Hampden Park.

It had been a heck of a journey, bur arguably these were the games that really put Rangers on the football map in Scotland.

TRIPLE CROWN NO.1

Rangers' first Triple Crown was also Scotland's first Triple Crown – no club had achieved the feat of winning the League, Scottish FA Cup and League Cup in the same season.

It happened in the 1948/49 – though in fairness the League Cup had only been in existence for two years!

Rangers' quest began with a 2-0 win over Raith Rovers in the final of the League Cup and with things going well in the League, there was optimism that this might be a special season.

That feeling increased as Rangers eased through the rounds in the Scottish Cup and completed the domestic cup double with a 4-1 win over Clyde in the final.

Suddenly, all eyes were on the Light Blues – could they add the League title to their haul and complete a first treble?

An excellent run of form in the last few weeks of the season saw Rangers go into the final game in second spot, a point behind leaders Dundee.

On paper, it was Dundee's title to lose as they were away to bottom of the table Albion Rovers while the Gers were at fifth-placed Falkirk.

On an extraordinary final day, Dundee completely lost their nerve and were thrashed 4-1 by relegated Albion while Rangers cruised to a 4-1 win at Falkirk to confirm their first domestic treble.

TRIPLE CROWN NO.2

The 1963/64 season was memorable enough for Rangers fans who saw their heroes beat Celtic five times from the five meetings that campaign, but it was the bigger picture that would go into the history books.

Rangers had a team packed with ability and talent that reached its peak this year, and as always, the League Cup was the first trophy up for grabs and Rangers deservedly lifted the trophy, thrashing Morton 5-0 in front of more than 105,000 fans at Hampden.

The Light Blues saw off Celtic on the way to the Scottish Cup final with 84,724 fans witnessing a 2-0 Ibrox win for the hosts.

Dundee, who had pushed Rangers hard on all fronts in recent years, were the opposition in the final and in a cracking game watched by a crowd of 120,982, Rangers edged home 3-1.

The league triumph was far more comfortable than the first treble achievement some 15 years before with the title wrapped up several weeks before the end of the season – the Gers ending top by six points.

The only failure – as such – was a first round European Cup exit at the hands of Real Madrid – ah well, you can't win them all!

1970

TRIPLE CROWN NO.3

The third occasion Rangers managed a domestic clean sweep was in the 1975/76 season, some 12 years after the last treble and 27 years since the first.

The Gers had finally broken a decade or so of Celtic domination by winning a first title in 11 years the season before and so went into the very first Scottish Premier League campaign in confident mood. An opening day win over Celtic at Ibrox proved the perfect start for the Light Blues who powered on from there.

October brought the first trophy as Rangers again defeated Celtic, this time by 1-0 to claim the League Cup and though the league form had been somewhat up and down up to that point, an unbeaten run of 26 games in league and Scottish Cup kept the Triple Crown on course.

Rangers would win the league by six points – the same margin as the last time they had done the treble so the Scottish Cup was the final piece of the jigsaw.

After reaching the final tie at Hampden Park, only Hearts stood in the way of Rangers completing a treble of Triple Crowns but after the Light Blues opened the scoring in the opening minute, the result was never in doubt and Hearts were beaten 3-1.

BATTLES WITH LEEDS

In March 1968 Rangers were paired with one of England's strongest sides, Leeds United, in the quarter-finals of the Fairs Cup – the forerunner for the UEFA Cup (now the Europa League).

It was the toughest draw the Light Blues could have got and the Yorkshire side proved a big draw at Ibrox with 80,000 witnessing a hard-fought 0-0 draw.

The return at Elland Road was watched by more than 51,000 fans, but two goals in three first-half minutes from Johnny Giles and Peter Lorimer (a Scot!) was enough for Leeds to secure a 2-0 win and Don Revie's side would go on to win the trophy.

The Gers had to wait 24 years for revenge when they drew Leeds again, this time in the European Cup Second Round.

This time, the first leg was at Ibrox but when Gary McAllister gave Leeds a first-minute lead, things looked bleak. But a John Lukic own goal and another from Ally McCoist before the break gave Rangers a narrow 2-1 win.

Although Leeds started as marginal favourites in the second leg, goals from Mark Hateley and McCoist put Rangers 2-0 up at Elland Road and although Eric Cantona pulled one back late on, it was too little, too late and Rangers marched on.

Rangers' shortest ever season lasted just five games and for good reason.

The Gers had started as though they meant business, beating St Mirren 5-1 at Ibrox in early August and watched by a crowd of 35,000.

A trip to Ayr United the following weekend resulted in a 4-0 victory for the Light Blues whose next match was also on the road – a 0-0 draw at Love Street against St Mirren who had clearly learned their lesson after the opening day thrashing!

Arbroath were next to suffer as Rangers coasted to a 3-1 win and a narrow 2-1 win over Third Lanark put the Gers top of Scottish Division One.

But the spectre of war hung heavy over the country after Germany's invasion of Poland the day before and the decision to suspend league football was take on 3rd September 1939.

Six years followed without regular football and Old Firm games were kept to lower crowds because of the possibility of aerial assault by the Germans, particularly with the Govan Shipyards close by.

Thankfully, the war ended in 1945 and league football resumed and regular league football resumed in 1946/47.

LET THERE BE LIGHT!

With floodlights offering new and exciting opportunities for football clubs to play night matches (or have the chance to see the finish clearly on a dark, wintry Scottish afternoon!), teams up and down Britain began to have them installed.

The new lighting towers meant that cup and league games could be played in the middle of the week, all with their own unique atmosphere that you just didn't get on a normal Saturday game.

The floodlights were a thing of beauty and awe to impressed supporters, especially children and Rangers installed them during the 1953/54 season.

The only way to sample a game under the lights at that point was to arrange a special match, so many clubs invited teams they had a good relationship with or even overseas opposition for this historic fixture.

Rangers invited old friends Arsenal to Glasgow for the inaugural floodlit game and on 8th December 1953, 69,256 fans turned out for a 'British Championship' clash with the Gunners.

It was the Londoners who emerged triumphant, winning the game 2-1 and the first Scottish league game wasn't played under lights for another three years in March 1956.

Rangers first real 'bad boy' was Willie Woodburn who was a Rangers player for 16 years.

A tough, uncompromising centre-back, Woodburn took no prisoners during his 216 games for the Gers.

His disciplinary record was poor and it eventually caught up with him. The war cost him seven years of his career having made his debut in 1938 but he was in hot water shortly after the resumption of league football.

Woodburn was banned for 14 days after a 'violent exchange' with a Motherwell player and in 1953 he was banned for 21 days after punching Clyde striker Billy McPhail.

Things got worse later that year when he was sent off for retaliation against Stirling and when the teams met the following season, Woodburn – already carrying an injury – was on the end of a bad foul and decided to take justice into his own hands, head-butting the perpetrator.

A month later, the SFA disciplinary took just a few minutes to ban Woodburn for life from playing football. It was harsh, but the authorities had just about had enough of bad boy Willie.

Three years later, the ban was lifted but at the age of 37, it was too late for the Rangers hard man to resume his career and he instead pursued the more gentle profession of becoming a journalist.

Rangers and Arsenal have been close allies for many years and played numerous friendlies.

In all there have been 23 games – none official – though several have been in pre-season tournaments. The first game was at Ibrox in 1933/34 and the last was in 2009 with the 1930s and 1950s producing a total of 11 matches.

There were five more friendlies played in the 1960s, but thereafter the fixtures became less often, though the bond between the clubs remains strong to this day.

Rangers have the slightly better record and the overall stats are: Played: 23 Won: 10 Drawn: 5 Lost: 8 For: 41 Against: 36

1933/34 Rangers 2, Arsenal 0 (Ibrox)
1933/34 Arsenal 1, Rangers 3 (Highbury)
1934/35 Arsenal 1, Rangers 1 (Highbury)
1935/36 Rangers 2, Arsenal 2 (Ibrox)
1936/37 Arsenal 2, Rangers 1 (Highbury)
1938/39 Rangers 1, Arsenal 0 (Ibrox)
1951/52 Arsenal 3, Rangers 2 (Highbury)
1953/54 Rangers 1, Arsenal 2 (Ibrox)
1954/55 Arsenal 3, Rangers 3 (Highbury)
1955/56 Rangers 2, Arsenal 0 (Ibrox)
1958/59 Arsenal 0, Rangers 3 (Highbury)
1960/61 Rangers 4, Arsenal 2 (Ibrox)
1962/63 Arsenal 2, Rangers 2 (Highbury)

1966/67 Rangers 2, Arsenal 0 (Ibrox)
1967/68 Arsenal 3, Rangers 0 (Highbury)
1968/69 Rangers 2, Arsenal 2 (Ibrox)
1973/74 Rangers 1, Arsenal 2 (Ibrox)
1980/81 Rangers 2, Arsenal 0 (Ibrox)
1989/90 Rangers 1, Arsenal 2 (Ibrox)
1996/97 Rangers 3, Arsenal 0 (Ibrox)
1996/97 Arsenal 3, Rangers 3 (Highbury)
2003/04 Rangers 0, Arsenal 3 (Ibrox)

Emirates Cup:
2nd August 2009: Arsenal 3 Rangers 0

FACT 62

There were a number of firsts on 24th October 1956 when Rangers took on Nice in the first round of the European Cup.

It was the Gers' first official game in European competition and the first leg was eagerly anticipated by the 65,000 Ibrox faithful.

It was the French side who scored the first goal, with a Jacques Faivre effort on 23 minutes, but the Light Blues fought back when Maxwell Murray wrote his name into the history books with an equaliser on 40 minutes.

William Simpson grabbed the winner on 81 minutes to give Rangers the edge in the first leg. The return in France was a feisty affair.

John Hubbard put Rangers ahead on 40 minutes, but on 61 and 64 minutes, Nice scored twice to turn the tie on its head. Both teams were then reduced to ten men after 81 minutes but the game ended 2-1 to Nice and 3-3 on aggregate.

That meant a play-off game to decide matters and Nice went on to win 3-1 in a match played in Paris. Rangers adventure was over and Nice were knocked out by Real Madrid.

CAPTAIN CUTLASS

Bobby Shearer was a swashbuckling right-back who represented Rangers between 1955 and 1965.

Having arrived at Ibrox from Hamilton Academicals, he played 267 times and 165 of those were in successive matches. The fans nicknamed the marauding defender 'Captain Cutlass' but Shearer's most famous moment came when the Light Blues travelled to Edinburgh in October 1960.

The Tynecastle fans must have thought it was going to be their day when Rangers keeper Billy Ritchie was injured after just 10 minutes.

With no subs allowed, Shearer took over in goal with still 80 minutes to play.

With the majority of the 30,000 crowd urging Hearts on, Rangers gave a backs to the wall performance that had the travelling fans in raptures.

By the end of the game, Shearer was the hero after the Gers recorded a stirring 3-1 win.

Shearer played for Scotland four times while with Rangers including a 9-3 defeat to England but it was that game at Hearts that Gers never forgot.

COINING IT IN

If you think penalties are a cruel way to lose a game, Rangers European Cup Winners' Cup quarter-final with Real Zaragoza proved there is an ever harsher method to decide a match.

Let's track back a little.

Rangers began their quest for a first European trophy in 1966/67 with a tie against Northern Irish side Glentoran.

After a 1-1 draw in the first leg, the Gers thrashed their British opponents 4-0 at Ibrox to progress to the next round.

As there were only 16 teams to begin with, that meant a quarter-final place against Spaniards Real Zaragoza with the Light Blues securing a 2-0 victory at Ibrox.

The second leg saw Zaragoza level the aggregate with a 2-0 victory, meaning extra time had to be played. The Gers were awarded a spot-kick four minutes in – but missed! With no penalties to decide the game, the match was to be decided on corners, but as this was also equal, the only option was the dreaded coin toss!

Rangers skipper John Grieg called tails, the referee flicked up the coin, caught it and revealed it was indeed tails – Rangers were through!

Rangers saw off Slavia Sofia by winning both legs 1-0 but were beaten by Bayern Munich in the final – the Germans' first European trophy!

TREBLE NO. 4

The 1977/78 season brought Rangers their fourth Triple Crown.

The season couldn't have started much worse having lost 3-1 to Aberdeen on the opening day and then been beaten 2-0 by Hibs a week later – hardly the form of champions!

A laboured 1-0 win over Swiss side Young Boys hardly inspired optimism but things steadily improved, though by the end of September, the Gers were dumped out of Europe by FC Twente.

With the league form improving dramatically, Rangers began to think about another hat-trick of trophies after beating Celtic 2-1 in the Scottish League Cup final.

A minor blip of one defeat and two draws was a set-back in the league, but after dispatching Dundee United in the Scottish Cup semi-final, the treble grew ever closer.

Four wins from the final four matches saw Rangers just edge home to the title, two points clear of Aberdeen who had pushed the Light Blues all the way.

But if the Dons hadn't suffered enough, they were also beaten 2-1 by Rangers in the Scottish Cup final on the last day of the campaign which gave Rangers a fourth treble and cap another memorable campaign.

OH DEAR...

Rangers endured a miserable 1983/84 season with the Club setting a new unwanted record.

Just one point from a possible 12 had some fans wondering if Rangers could actually be on their way to a relegation fight, but a 6-3 win over St Johnstone in game No.5 eased immediate concern.

In fact, that win was the start of 23 goals in just four games as Gers went goal crazy in just 11 days, but it was the calm before the storm.

The Light Blues then embarked on their worst league run of defeats starting with a 3-2 loss at Dundee and then a 2-1 home loss to Motherwell.

After St Mirren inflicted a 3-0 loss at Love Street, it was followed by a 2-1 Old Firm loss at Ibrox as the Gers' poor run continued.

The misery was completed with a 3-0 thrashing at Aberdeen – a record five straight losses for the first time in the club's history.

The run ended with a 0-0 draw against Dundee United and Rangers rallied embarking on a run of just one loss in 24 games s to end the season in fourth, 15 points adrift of champions Aberdeen.

A Scottish League Cup final win over Celtic also helped lift the gloom!

BACK IN A MO?

Mo Johnston's career was plagued by controversy, though almost entirely at club level in this particular instance. A rare beast indeed, Mo Johnston was a natural goal-scorer and therefore coveted by both club and country.

Glasgow-born Johnston made his name with Partick Thistle and won his first Scotland cap in 1984 against Wales, aged 20, scoring in a 2-1 win. A subsequent move south to Watford followed prior to Johnston returning home where he became a huge crowd favourite with Celtic during the mid-Eighties, before moving on to French side Nantes for two years.

Despite claiming he wouldn't return to Scottish club football, he seemed set for an emotional return to Parkhead in 1989 – only to sign for Rangers in one of the most dramatic transfer twists in SPL history.

He was tagged the 'highest profile Roman Catholic signing' since the first world and some Rangers fans threatened to burn their season tickets in protest. Despite the vilification from Celtic supporters, he stayed at Ibrox for two years and his stock rose sharply when he scored an injury-time winner against Celtic.

His two years at Ibrox resulted in 31 goals from 76 games before he moved on again, this time to Everton.

TRIPLE CROWN NO.5

Rangers won their fifth domestic sweep in 1992/93 in what would prove to be yet another historic campaign in the club's history.

A 2-1 win Scottish League Cup win over Aberdeen started the cycle at the end of October and shortly after the Light Blues beat Leeds United to qualify for the newly-formed Champions League group stage for the first time.

Indeed, the Gers were impressive throughout the group stage, remaining unbeaten in six games but failing to qualify because Marseille just edged the top spot.

The Scottish Cup was progressing well though and a 2-1 win over Hearts set up a final on the final day of the campaign.

Gers comfortably wrapped up the SPL title, cruising home nine points ahead of Aberdeen who must have been sick of the sight of the Ibrox giants – but it was about to get worse!

Rangers again clinched the Scottish Cup and again beat Aberdeen 2-1 to secure a fifth domestic treble – as for the Dons, they had to write 'runners-up to Rangers' three times in their history books that season!

CELTIC SPOIL THE PARTY!

Rangers came so close to setting a new Scottish top tier title record in 1997/98, but arch rivals Celtic ruined everything!

The Gers had dominated Scottish football for nine seasons, winning the SPL every season to equal Celtic's record of nine successive championships.

One more would mean 10 in a row and a new record to make Rangers fans even prouder of their club – plus a chance to rub Celtic's noses in the mud a little!

With two games to go, Celtic and Rangers were neck and neck at the top with virtually everything the same in terms of goals, wins, draws and points – but crucially, Rangers were one point clear and two wins would guarantee a record tenth successive title.

Rangers went into their final two matches confident they could see the job over the line – but there was to be heartbreak.

After missing at least two fantastic chances to score against Kilmarnock – one chance being virtually an open net for Ally McCoist - it was to be another Ally who score the only goal in the dying moments – Kilmarnock's Ally Mitchell.

A 1-0 home loss allowed Celtic to go two points clear and a final day win at Dundee United was not enough to repair the damage and Celtic ended up champions by two points.

The Gers then lost the Scottish Cup Final to Hearts a week later to complete a thoroughly miserable end to the campaign.

ONE GOAL CONCEDED
AND THE ORANGE FINAL

The 1999/2000 campaign saw Rangers only manage a league and cup double!

The Gers secured the title with a record points haul of 90, finishing 21 points clear of second-placed Celtic after a stunning SPL campaign that saw 96 goals scored.

The Gers were far and away the best team in Scotland with the only disappointment being that a seventh Triple Crown wasn't secured – the Light Blues went out of the Scottish League Cup at the quarter-final stage to (later to be relegated) Aberdeen.

Rangers breezed through the rounds of the Scottish Cup, beating St Johnstone 2-0 and Morin 1-0 to reach the last eight.

There they faced – and thrashed – Hearts 4-1 to set up a semi-final with Ayr United, but it turned into an embarrassing day for Ayr as the Gers romped home 7-0.

For the final against Aberdeen, Rangers fans wanted to show their appreciation to manager Dick Advocaat by making the occasion an 'Oranje Day' in a tribute to their Dutch boss.

Hampden Park was a sight to behold with the majority of the 50, 865 crowd decked in orange – the colours of the Dutch national team – and the players rose to the occasion, beating the Dons 4-0.

It may have seemed a fairly normal day as Rangers beat Dundee United at Tannadyce 2-0.

This was the first season when teams were awarded three points for a win and while the Gers coasted towards yet another SPL title, Dundee United were slipping out of the top flight after a rotten campaign.

So what happened that was special on April fool's Day 1995?

Gordon Durie is the answer. The Scotland forward set a new club record when he opened the scoring with just 10 seconds on the clock – the fastest Rangers goals ever scored.

For Durie it was at the start of a very successful spell at Ibrox as he was a key part of the team that was in the middle of a run that would land nine successive titles.

Durie had made his name South of the Border in England with Chelsea and Tottenham before returning home to lead the Rangers line.

He would win seven titles with the Light Blues in total and his career high was a hat-trick against Hearts in the 1996 Scottish Cup Final.

He remained at the club from 1993 until 2000, returning as assistant manager in 2014-15.

His record still stands some 21 years after he set it and will take some beating!

TRIPLE CROWN NO.6

With the 1997/98 campaign ending trophyless – a very rare occurrence indeed in Rangers history – new boss Dick Advocat knew he had to produce the goods for his second season in charge.

A repeat of the previous year would almost certainly mean the sack, but he needn't have worried as the Gers stormed back into top gear.

Despite losing the opening SPL game against Hearts, the Light Blues then embarked on an unbeaten run of 18 games as they set out their stall for the coming months.

Despite losing 5-1 to Celtic in the league and being knocked out of the UEFA Cup by Parma within the space of a few weeks, sandwiched in-between was a Scottish League Cup win over St Johnstone and thereafter the Gers set off on another explosive run that saw them win 13 games and draw one, demolishing teams right left and centre.

A 3-0 win over Celtic at the start of May virtually guaranteed the title would be coming back to Ibrox and Rangers would eventually win the SPL by six points.

The Gers then completed their sixth domestic clean sweep by beating Celtic 1-0 in the Scottish Cup and round off a superb campaign.

Rangers became the first Scottish club to progress past the Champions League group stages in 2005/06 – another notable first for the club.

The journey began with a Third Qualifying Round tie against Cypriot side Anorthosis Famagusta with Rangers winning 2-1 in Cyprus and 2-0 at Ibrox to progress through to the group stage.

Things started well with a 3-2 win over Porto but a 1-0 defeat away to Inter Milan was an early blow.

Two points were dropped at home to Artmedia Bratislava after a dour 0-0 draw and the teams drew again in the return, this time 2-2.

In a tight group Rangers then took a creditable 1-1 draw away to Porto before hosting Italian giants Inter at Ibrox, a game that again ended in a draw – a fourth in succession as the team tied 1-1.

Normally, seven points would not be enough to finish in the top two, but this time it was, meaning Rangers were now in the Round of 16 for the first time.

Pitted against La Liga side Villarreal, the Gers twice fought back from behind to draw 2-2 at Ibrox.

The return game saw Peter Lovenkrands put the Gers ahead early in the game, but the Spanish side, nicknamed 'The Yellow Submarine' equalised to draw 1-1 and go through on away goals.

There has never been a more dramatic or joyous end to a season than the 2004/05 campaign.

It was Celtic's title to lose – but somehow, lose it they did!

With one game to go, Celtic were two points clear with a trip to Motherwell to come while Rangers were away to Hibernian.

Though neither fixture was easy, both teams were expected to win, few could have predicted the

drama that lay in store.

On 29 minutes, Celtic went ahead in their game, putting them five points clear in the 'live' league table. That, it seemed, was game, set and match.

The Gers were toiling against Hibs, unable to put any pressure on their great rivals but just before the hour-mark, Nacho Novo scored to give Rangers a 1-0 lead.

With a far better goal difference, if Motherwell did equalise against Celtic, the Gers would go top.

But with 89 minutes gone at both games, it seemed Celtic had done just about enough – then Ibrox erupted! Scott McDonald had levelled for Motherwell and the celebrations began – unless Celtic managed to find a goal in the time that remained.

Then came the news that McDonald had scored his second in a minute to make it 2-1 – the news filtered through to the Rangers fans who went crazy – their old rivals had crumbled just as they were about to cross the finishing line and the Gers were champions again – incredible!

So why Helicopter Sunday? Well the rumour was the SPL trophy was going to be flown to the stadium of the champions and as Motherwell scored their second, commentator Peter Martin told viewers 'The helicopter is changing direction!' Enough said!

MOST THRILLING FINISH

Rangers' task at the start of the 2002/03 season was simple – stop Celtic winning a third successive SPL title.

Not only did the Gers manage this, but they added an unprecedented seventh Triple Crown in what turned out to be one of the most exciting finishes in the club's history.

Both clubs were dominating the SPL and going into the final weekend, had both won 30 of their 37 games, drawn four matches and lost three.

That put both sides on 94 points – but with one game left, each had identical goal differences of +68. It was, in effect, a one-game shoot-out with the team winning by the biggest margin crowned champions.

Neither task was easy on paper with Rangers at home to fifth-placed Dunfermline and Celtic away to fourth-placed Kilmarnock.

Gers had met Dunfermline six times already that season, winning five and drawing the other but almost 50,000 Ibrox fans held their breath as both Rangers and Celtic kicked off.

The day's events would see both sides topping the live SPL table, but it was to be Rangers' day, winning 6-1 against Dunfermline while Celtic – who won 4-0 but missed a penalty and hit the post – just fell short by one goal.

With the Scottish League Cup already secured after a win over Celtic, a 1-0 Scottish Cup win over Dundee completed a season to remember.

SHORTEST REIGN

Paul Le Guen holds the unwanted record of shortest managerial reign for Rangers.

Former France boss Le Guen took over for the 2006/07 season but made a poor start to his first campaign at Ibrox with just five wins from the opening 13 matches the worst start to a season for 28 years.

Then Rangers were dumped out by First Division St Johnstone who triumphed 2-0 at Ibrox – the Light Blues' first home loss to a lower league side.

Defeats to Falkirk and Inverness CT before Christmas meant Rangers' hopes of the title were already fading and the blame was placed firmly at Le Guen's feet. Could the Frenchman turn the tide?

He couldn't have started the New Year any worse, stripping popular midfielder Barry Ferguson of the captaincy and dropping him after a fall-out – but the move backfired, Ferguson refused to play foe Le Guen again and on 4th January the manager left Ibrox by 'mutual consent'.

He was the first manager to leave part-way through a season and his overall record reflected a season of struggle.

Just 16 wins from 31 games is not good enough for a Rangers boss and his six-month reign ended with a 1-0 win over Motherwell.

THIRD CLASS CITIZENS?

There were plenty of new records created in season 2012/13 – many of them unwanted!

Rangers were playing outside the top division for the first time in the club's history having been demoted by the Scottish FA for going into liquidation and having unpaid taxes.

That meant the Scottish Third Division and Peterhead, Elgin City and Forres Mechanics for the Light Blues rather than Celtic, Aberdeen and Hearts.

Rangers knew that if they had three back-to-back promotions, they could be back in the SPL and back where they belong, but there would be hiccups along the way.

Some believed Rangers would win every league game in 2012/13, but it wasn't as straightforward as that and a narrow opening day 2-1 win over Brechin City was a taste of things to come.

Draws against Peterhead and Berwick made August an uncomfortable month but Gers remained unbeaten in their opening 13 league and cup matches – before Stirling Albion finally created their own history by securing a 1-0 win at the Forthbank Stadium.

That seemed to shake the Light Blues into life and they then recorded 11 wins on the bounce to race clear at the top but though things went well until March, a 2-1 home defeat to Annan at Ibrox was an embarrassing loss.

Peterhead also won at Ibrox a few weeks later but Rangers still ran out comfortable champions and the 50,048 fans that crammed into Ibrox for the final day of the season against Berwick was a world record crowd for a fourth tier game.

FACT 78

Rangers followed their first ever season in the Scottish Third Division with a first ever season in the Scottish League One.

A reshuffle between the Scottish FA and the SPL meant the Scottish Second was now League One – but still the third tier of Scottish football.

While the Gers may have not been taking on the cream of the crop, it still proved to be a fantastic season on many levels.

Of their 36 league games, the Light Blues would win 33 matches and draw the other three as they cruised home with a winning margin of 39 points over second placed Dunfermline Athletic.

Rangers racked up 102 points and scored 106 goals along the way. The unbeaten run included three games from the previous campaign for a new record of 39 matches without defeat.

The Gers were now just one season away from a fast-track return to the top division – though it would take two seasons in the Championship before the Gers did return to the SPL.

DaMarcus Beasley may not have been the greatest Rangers player to have ever served the club, but he did manage to get into the record books.

Beasley moved to Ibrox from PSV Eindhoven in June 2007 after spending a season on loan with Manchester City.

The pacey winger would go on to spend three years in Scotland, playing 46 matches and scoring seven goals.

He was part of the team that won two titles plus the Scottish League Cup and Scottish Cup but he was never a regular starter and missed a number of games through injury.

So why is he in the 100 Rangers Facts book?

Well Beasley is the most capped player to play for the club with 114 appearances for the USA.

To date he has won a staggering 132 United States caps and while he may not be in many top ten favourites lists of supporters, he made a mark during his time with the Gers.

Ally McCoist holds the record of most caps earned while a Rangers player, with 59 caps for Scotland.

CLUB CREST

Rangers have one of football's most recognisable club crests with the intertwined RFC motif simple and effective.

It is believed to date back to 1872, though the earliest proof of the crest being used was in the 1881/82 season and would remain in place for 70 years.

The crest changed to a circular badge with 'Ready' written in from 1959 until 1968 when the original design returned and was placed on the shirts for the first time.

There have been minor tweaks over the years but in 1997/98 the crest was put into a shield design for the first time.

Perhaps the most significant change came in 2003/04 after Rangers had clinched a 50th top flight title – the decision was made to add five stars above the badge, each one representing ten title triumphs.

INTERNATIONAL GERS

Some 41 different nationalities have represented Rangers at some stage with some more surprising than others.

In alphabetical order, two Algerians have played for the club as well as five Australian; there have been one each from Bosnia and Belgium. Two from Canada, one from Chile, two from Croatia and one from the Czech Republic.

There have been five Danish players, one Egyptian – just seven from England – and two from Finland. France has provide two, Gabon one, Georgia two and one German.

One Greek, one Honduran, one Icelandic and seven from Ireland have all played for Rangers and there have been two Lithuanians, one Nigerian and nine Dutch stars, no less!

Northern Ireland has provided nine players, Norway two while Poland and Portugal have just one each. Two Romanians, one Russian and two each from Serbians, Slovakians and South African.

There have been three Swedes, two from Trinidad & Tobago, two Tunisians and one from Turkey as well as two Ukrainians and four Americans – phew!

CHAIRMEN

There was a time when a Rangers Chairman would spend many years in the post, effectively making the decisions that shaped the club – but in recent years it has become something of a poisoned chalice, with Chairmen coming and going like cars at a drive through!

The club's first Chairman was James Henderson – prior to that the club secretary was regarded as the main man. Henderson held his post for 13 years between 1899 and 1912 before Sir John Ure Primrose took the post for the next 11 years.

William Crag was briefly appointed in 1923 but Joseph Buchanan took the post that same year and held it until 1932.

Duncan Graham lasted two years but his successor, James Bowie, lasted 13. William Simpson was at the helm from 1947 to 1949 and then John F Wilson took charge from 1947 to 1963 – a 16-year stint.

John Lawrence then came in for 10 years, followed by Matthew Taylor (1973-75) and Rae Simpson who was the top man for nine years,

John Paton lasted two years, David Holmes three before Sir David Murray arrived for a 13-year stint.

John McLelland lasted a couple of years before Murray returned for another five (making 18 years in total – comfortably the most) and between 2009 and the present day there have been seven in six years!

Former Liverpool and Scotland star Graeme Souness had an explosive effect on Rangers both on and off the pitch.

The fiery hard man became the Gers' player-manager in 1986 and was charged with the task of ending a nine-year spell of no titles for the club in one of the bleakest spells in Rangers history.

Souness used his contacts from the English league to attract several big-name England stars in Terry Butcher, Trevor Steven and Chris Woods as he shaped a side capable of winning the SPL.

With a reputation for being a tough, uncompromising midfielder, Souness allowed his passion to boil over on his debut against Hibs after he was sent off for an altercation during the game. He also received a three-match ban and a £500 fine.

While it wasn't the kind of start Souness had wanted, it did stir his players to find the spirit and determination that had been missing for so long.

By the end of the campaign, Souness had guided the Light Blues to the title, ending that nine year jinx and the Scottish League Cup was also won after a 2-1 win over Celtic.

Souness would win two more titles in the next two seasons before returning to Liverpool to become the Reds' manager – he left having turned the club's fortunes around and a sequence of nine titles on the bounce.

FINAL FURY

Rangers reached their fifth successive Scottish Cup final in 1979/80 but the game against Celtic would be remembered for all the wrong reasons.

In a tense game that Rangers deserved to win, the match ended 0-0 after 90 minutes and so went into extra time.

Played in front of more than 70,000 fans at Hampden Park, the Hoops took the lead when George McCluskey turned a cross from Celtic's Danny McGrain into his own net.

The Celtic fans' celebrations were exuberant and their fans started to spill on the pitch, a few at first and then hundreds which provoked Rangers fans to also come on to the pitch, ending in a mass brawl.

Mounted police finally cleared the pitch but the disgraceful scenes meant steps needed to be taken and as a result, alcohol was banned at all Scottish grounds – a ban that has remained in place to the present day – it was a dark day in the history of the Old Firm clubs.

RANGERS LADIES

Rangers Ladies have only been in existence since 2008 and going into the 2016/17 season, they were yet to win a major title.

The team began life as Arthurlie Ladies but became Paisley City Ladies in 1999. After struggling financially, they became Rangers Ladies in order to survive as the Gers followed in the footsteps of Aberdeen, Celtic and Hibernian in developing a women's team.

Rangers Ladies replaced Paisley City in the Scottish Women's Frist Division with many Paisley players joining Rangers as a result.

The Gers Ladies won their division at the first attempt and also reached the Scottish Women's Cup final where they lost 5-0 to Glasgow City and reached the final again in 2010, losing 2-1 to Hibs.

In 2014 Rangers Ladies finished second in the Women's Premier League – the highest finish yet at the team continues to progress.

One of Rangers most famous and controversial signings was Paul Gascoigne, better known as 'Gazza'. An undoubted footballing genius, as colourful off the pitch as he was on it – often led to front page newspaper headlines.

After successful spells at Newcastle, Tottenham and Lazio, Gazza joined Rangers in 1995 for a club record fee of £4.3m. He became an instant hero after just five matches when he ran the length of the pitch to score a superb goal against Celtic.

Always one to have fun, when the ref dropped a yellow card in one game, Gazza picked it up and showed it to him – and was duly booked for his cheek!

But with a ball at his feet, Gazza was even more entertaining and he inspired the Light Blues to success, scoring a hat-trick in the penultimate game against Aberdeen to clinch the title. He scored 19 goals in 42 games that season and was voted the PFA Scotland Players' Player of the Year as a result.

Gazza was again inspirational during his second campaign, scoring two hat-tricks and 17 goals in 34 games as the Gers recorded their ninth successive SPL title. Earlier in the season Gazza had scored twice in a 4-3 Scottish League Cup win over Celtic.

His third season was littered with controversy, bans and fines and he was less effective on the team's fortunes, scoring 3 in 17 matches before joining Middlesbrough in 1998.

With 39 goals in 104 games plus four major trophies, Paul Gascoigne is still fondly remembered by Rangers fans.

SCOTTISH SPORTS
HALL OF FAME

Three Rangers players have made it to the Scottish Sports Hall of Fame since it was set up in 2002.

Covering 25 major sports and one multi-sports section, the Hall of Fame was created to recognise Scotland's finest sports men and women.

Up to 2015, 98 sports starts had been inducted and Rangers players account for three of those slots.

Jim Baxter, who had two spells at Ibrox and won 34 caps for Scotland. Baxter was a gifted left sided midfielder, supremely skilled and an entertaining player.

John Grieg was also honoured by being inducted. Grieg spent 17 years with Rangers and is widely regarded as the greatest Rangers player of all time and it was no surprise that he was included.

Finally, Ally McCoist, the record goal-scorer for Rangers is the third player from the Light Blues to be honoured in the Scottish Sports Hall of Fame.

Hopefully, there will be many more Rangers players inducted in future years.

UNLUCKY FOR SOME?

Rangers have achieved their record score not once, not twice but on three occasions – not bad when you consider that record score is 13-0.

The victories all came within the space of two goal-crazy years between 1887 and 1889 and have all come in the Scottish Cup.

In 1887, Rangers first struck thirteen times as they put Possilpark to the sword and then recorded another 13-0 win over Uddingston in the same competition.

Two years later, Rangers thrashed Kelvinside 13-0 in 1889 to make it a triple whammy of 13 goals in the Scottish Cup.

The Light Blues have scored more goals in a game on two different occasions.

In 1883 Whitehill were destroyed 14-2 – again In the Scottish Cup – and in 1934, Blairgowrie went down 14-2 – also in the cup.

So why is it that those games are not the record victories? Well, it's all about margins and the 13-goal margins are obvious bigger that the 12-goal margin recorded in the 14-2 victories.

ENGLISH, THE IRISH SCOTSMAN!

Heard the one about the Northern Irish striker playing in Scotland by the name of English?

It's not an old joke, it actually happened with Sam English spending one prolific season at Ibrox in 1931/32.

English holds a number of club records from his two seasons with the Light Blues with his first campaign nothing short of incredible as the 23 year-old scored 54 goals in all competitions.

Among the many he scored, English bagged five against Morton, four against Queen's Park and a further seven hat-tricks scored against Dundee United, Leith Athletic, Falkirk, Brechin City, Ayr United and Raith Rovers.

English scored 44 league goals in 35 matches during his first season – a club record that has stood for 85 years.

He also scored in the Scottish Cup final that season, helping his team beat Kilmarnock 3-0 but his second season with the Gers was less successful with just 11 in 30 starts in all competitions.

English would leave the club in 1933 after a tragic accident resulted in the death of Celtic goalkeeper John Thomson who suffered head injuries when he collided with English's knee.

The Rangers man was cleared of all blame but he was never the same person again and though he played on, he retired at the age of 28 having never mentally recovered from the incident.

Although John Grieg officially holds the record of most games for Rangers, even the great man himself can't hold a candle to Dougie Gray's astonishing record.

Gray was the quintessential Rangers man, staying at Ibrox his entire career which lasted a staggering 22 years!

Gray began his career in 1925, after leaving the wonderfully named amateur side Aberdeen Muggiemoss for Glasgow.

The nimble but pacey full-back used brain over brawn and quickly became an integral part of the Light Blues' team.

A cultured defender – perhaps ahead of his time – Gray also had a speciality which was goal-line clearances. Many a striker was left cursing the Rangers defender as they prepared to celebrate a goal!

Gray would go on to win 10 Scottish League titles as well as six Scottish Cup triumphs and he continued to play for the club through the war years – and though these are considered 'unofficial games, by the time Gray retired in 1947, he'd played 940 matches for the Gers!

Capped 10 times by Scotland, long-serving boss Bill Struth claimed Gray was his 'best ever signing' – quite an accolade!

James Bowie certainly left his mark at Ibrox.

The wing-half joined Rangers in 1910 from Queen of the South and would go on to play more than 300 times for the Light Blues during a 12-year stay that was truncated by World War 1.

A creative inside forward, Bowie was a title winner five times before hanging his boots up in 1922, but his journey at the club continued as he took over the role of administrator in 1925 and then became chairman in 1934.

He held the post for 13 years but his time was up when he suggested that legendary boss Bill Struth should retire because he was 71!

Struth was considered untouchable by the club directors and so Bowie was sent packing, despite having racked up 37 years' service!

He served as President of the Scottish Football League from 1939 to 1946, overseeing a difficult time during World War 2.

He remains the only man to have served as player, director and chairman – a unique record that is unlikely to be broken anytime soon.

FIXED PENALTY NOTICE

Rangers once lost a game and then won it, all in the same evening!

Confused? You should be, but then so was everybody else.

On 3rd November 1971 Rangers were away to Sporting Lisbon in the European Cup Winners' Cup having won the first leg at Ibrox by 3-2.

The Portuguese side fought back in the second leg, also winning 3-2 and so sending the tie into extra time.

The Gers equalised on 100 minutes to make it 3-3 on the night and 6-5 overall, but on 114 minutes, Lisbon went into a 4-3 lead.

On full-time, the referee ordered a penalty shoot-out despite Rangers' players insisting to the official that they had actually won – you couldn't make it up!

Lisbon won the penalty shoot-out and their fans and players believed they had progressed to the quarter-finals.

The issue was the new away goals rule that had just been introduced – the ref clearly didn't understand but after a journalist pointed out to the Rangers boss Waddell that his team had, in fact won and after consulting UEFA officials, it was confirmed.

Of course, Rangers went on to win the trophy – their only European success to date – and this game became part of club folklore as a result.

£30 OR BUST!

Rangers may never have become the club they eventually did but for George Goudie.

His name may not be as familiar as some from the Gers' history, but make no mistake, this was a very important man who stepped in at a time the Light Blues were in danger of going out of existence before they had even really got going.

Rangers didn't have a home of their own back in 1883 and had fallen into financial difficulties with their landlords at Kinning Park with little or no cash coming into the club – remember this was long before there was additional revenue from sponsors. TV deals or season-tickets.

An emergency meeting was called where Rangers' Treasurer Mr J Ness solemnly to the board members: "It has come to this - we must have £30 or we cannot carry on. There is not a farthing in the exchequer. Can anyone suggest where the £30 is to come from?"

It was then a hero stepped forward with club President, Mr George Goudie replying: "We cannot allow the club to go under without a fight, I shall advance the £30 – and let us all hope for better times."

Goudie advanced the cash – worth around £1,000 in today's money – and Rangers were able to not only continue, but prosper and become one of the most famous football clubs in the world.

Rangers have the unique record of being the first British club to play a European Cup tie in London – not bad for a team from Glasgow!

In the 1959-60 season Rangers had progressed to the quarter-finals of the competition having seen off Anderlecht 7-2 on aggregate and then narrowly edging past Cervena Hviezda Bratislava in the second round.

The Gers were twice behind at Ibrox in front of a crowd of more than 80,000 before winning the first leg 4-3 and then securing a 1-1 draw in Czechoslovakia to win 5-4 on aggregate.

The quarter-finals paired Rangers with Dutch side Sparta Rotterdam and in the first leg in Holland, it seemed the Gers were home and dry as they led 2-0 and 3-1 before conceding a late goal to make it 3-2.

With 85,000 packed into Ibrox for the return, all Rangers needed to do was see out the last few minutes to progress but an 82nd-minute goal for the visitors meant the tie ended 3-3.

With no penalties or the away goals rule to settle the tie, the match was replayed at Arsenal's Highbury stadium on 30th March 1960 and therefore became the first European Cup tie to be played in the English capital.

In an exciting play-off played in front of 34,178 fans, Rangers won 3-2 to move into the semi-final where they were thrashed 6-1 and 6-3 in the two legs played against German side Eintracht Frankfurt.

THE GREATEST RANGERS GOAL AT WEMBLEY?

Rangers are yet to play an official match at Wembley Stadium, either the old one or the new version.

Yet in 1996, the goal that was voted the greatest ever at Wembley, was scored and it involved two Rangers players.

It was Euro '96 and England were playing Scotland in a bid to top the group.

England were leading 1-0 through Alan Shearer, but Scotland were still in the game and had a chance to level when a penalty was awarded – but Gary McAllister saw his shot saved by David Seaman.

Moments later, Rangers favourite Paul Gascoigne picked up a pass in midfield, knocked it over the head of defender Colin Hendry before volleying a low shot past – you guessed it – Rangers keeper Andy Goram!

A goal made in Glasgow, though no Rangers fan or anyone else in Scotland was celebrating – except for Gazza!

Between 1891 and 1965, Rangers met Third Lanark on 116 occasions with the Gers winning 82 and drawing 18.

The last 11 meetings were all won by Rangers but in 1967, the Light Blues' Glasgow neighbours went out of business having been in existence for 95 years.

Lanark finished third in the top division in 1960/61 but their demise was quick and steady thereafter as they slipped through the divisions, losing money, players and fans.

Only 297 spectators turned out for one of their final games before they were officially wound up due to a hopeless financial situation.

Rangers played Third Lanark for the final time in 1965, beating them 5-0 at Ibrox.

There have been several attempts to revive the fortunes of Third Lanark including an Under-18s team, a ladies team and an amateur side was formed in 2008 with hopes of making it back into league football.

THE GREATEST COMEBACK?

The 1987 Old Firm clash at Ibrox will live long in the memory for all those who witnessed it.

It was explosive, packed with controversial moments, goals and red cards.

The drama began in the first half when Celtic's Frank McAvennie barged into Rangers keeper Chris Woods and the resulting altercation saw both players sent off.

That meant Graham Roberts, a central defender, had to go in goal for the Gers.

Roberts did his best but Andy Walker put Celtic ahead shortly after and before the break, Terry Butcher scored an own goal to make it 2-0 to Celtic.

All seemed lost when Butcher was sent off in the second half but somehow, nine-man Rangers fought back.

Ally McCoist made it 1-2 with a thumping shot off the post to give the home fans hope, but in the meantime, Celtic hit the underside of the crossbar and went close several times.

Then, with seconds remaining, a cross from Ian Durrant caused a scramble in the Celtic penalty area and Richard Gough managed to bundle home the equaliser.

To say Ibrox went crazy was an understatement – it was one of the loudest roars ever heard at the ground and somehow, Rangers had earned a remarkable 2-2 draw.

Rangers are one of European football's most experienced clubs having played in 313 matches up to the 2016/17 season.

Those games were spread across the Champions League (161 matches), the European Cup Winners' Cup (54), the Europa League/UEFA Cup (76), Super Cup (2) and Fairs Cup (18).

Of those games, 128 have been won, 80 drawn and 105 have ended in defeat.

Rangers have scored 461 goals and conceded 380 – the Champions League has seen the Gers lose most often with 59 losses from 161 games played – a win ratio of 38.51%

Germany has provided the most opponents, with 47 games against Bundesliga opponents in all competitions.

The Light Blues have faced French sides on 25 occasions, Italian opposition on 23 occasions and Spanish on 20.

Meeting teams from Denmark has resulted in five wins and a draw from six games – a win ratio of 83% - the highest success rate against any nation in Europe.

However, just one win in eight games against Greek opponents is the worst record of all, with a win rate of just 12.5%.

WHEN RANGERS
SAVED ARSENAL

In 1910 Arsenal, or Woolwich Arsenal as it was then known, saw its attempt to launch shares in the club collapse. It became widespread knowledge that the club was in such deep financial trouble that the League had demanded a meeting to ascertain if they would be able to continue the following season.

As rumours began to circulate abut the state of the club counter rumours were abound that Tottenham, Chelsea and Rangers were all trying to buy all or part of Woolwich Arsenal FC.

Eventually it was Rangers who came to Arsenal's aid, buying two shares at the time. Arsenal's manager, George Morrell, who had previously worked for Rangers wrote to them with an appeal for help. The shares cost Rangers £1 each. Twenty years later the London club handed Rangers 14 shares for free in gratitude for their help, cementing a lasting relationship between the two clubs.

Rangers continued to hold these shares until infamous owner Craig Whyte sold all 16 shares at a total price of £230,000 to wealthy Russian businessman Alisher Usmanov in 2012, much to the consternation of many people involved with Rangers who felt the shares should never have been sold, as a mark of the bond between the two clubs.

One of the most famous derby games in the world, Rangers v Celtic is a fixture like no other.

Fierce rivalry on and off the pitch and more than 125 years of battles mean there is no game quite like it.

It is also the lifeblood of Scottish football and the reason Glasgow has dominated football in

Scotland for more than 125 years.

From the first meeting in 1890, to the Scottish Cup tie in 2016, there have been 330 clashes of the Glasgow clans, most of them explosive!

To date, Rangers are comfortably ahead having won 132 of the derby games compared with Celtic's 111.

At Ibrox, Rangers have win 76 times, there have been 44 draws and Celtic have won 35 times. At Parkhead, the Hoops have won 73 times, there have been 45 Rangers wins and 43 draws.

Of the 14 games played on neutral ground, the Gers have won 11 and lost three and overall, Rangers have scored 465 times to Celtic's 433.

Rangers' record win is 5-0 from the 1893/94 season and Celtic's record Old Firm win is 6-2 in 2000.

Between April 2012 and February 2015, the teams didn't play at all due to Rangers' demotion from the top division – but in 2016/17, the battle resumed again in the SPL, and long may it continue.

The 100 Facts Series